Disloyal Yo-Yo

Disloyal Yo-Yo

Bruce Cohen

Dream Horse Press
California

Library of Congress Cataloging-in-Publication Data:

Cohen, Bruce
Disloyal Yo-Yo
p. cm

ISBN 978-0-9821155-3-4
1. Poetry

10 9 8 7 6 5 4 3 2 1

First Edition

Cover: "Parade" by Gail Marcus-Orlen

Contents

Disloyal Yo-Yo

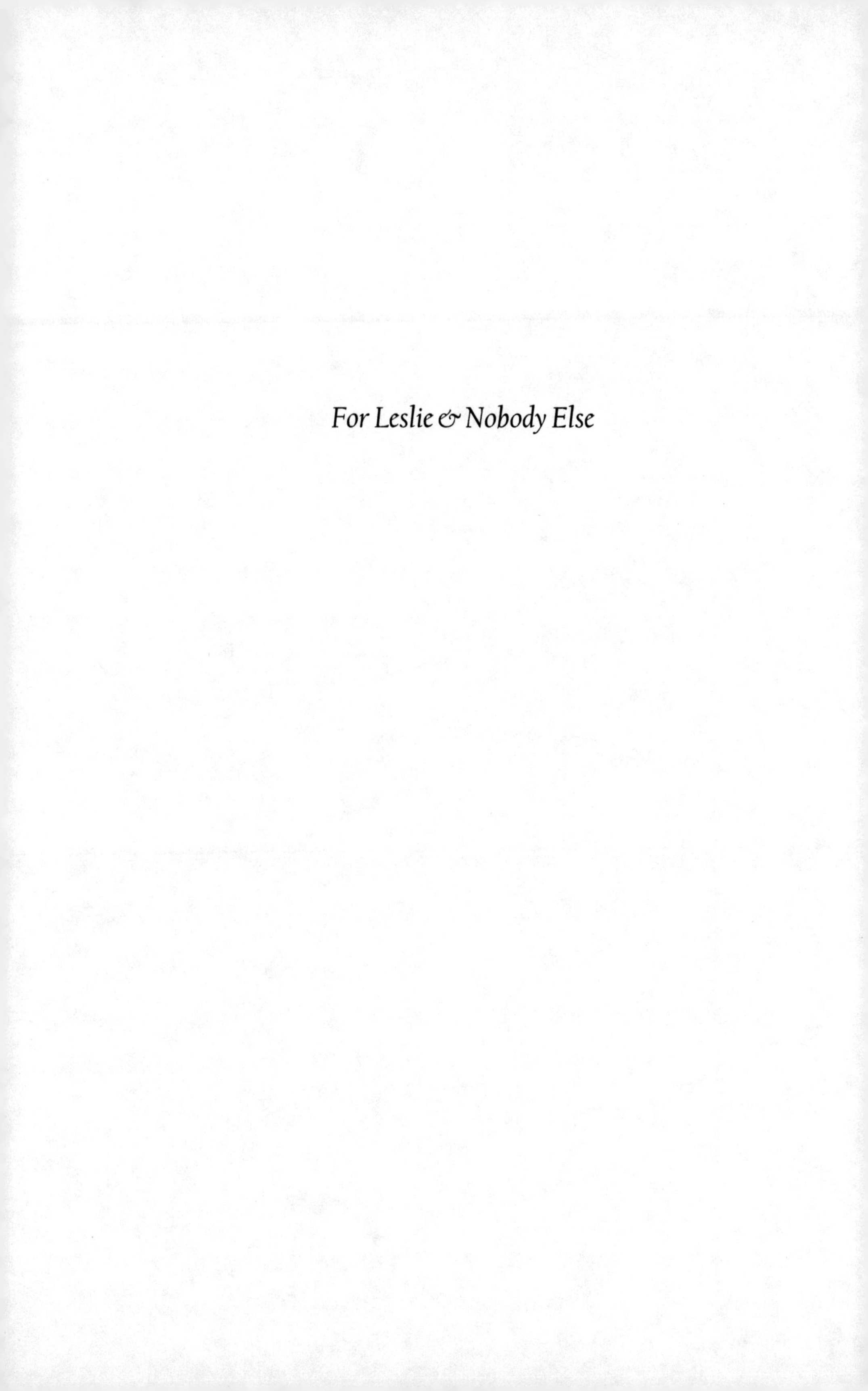

For Leslie & Nobody Else

Sober Trees

Days I don't drink I am aimless
in a crowded Sears in a small Iowa.

The lights are ridiculously bright
& frankly, I can't get used to that.

I am mesmerized with the escalators
& not just the oblivious ups & downs

but by the illusion of not getting any-
where & continuously. I drink strategic-

-ally half the time to be unsure of my natural
state of consciousness. It's a pillow over

the face this sober thing. In its parking
lot, the vulture tow trucks look for souls

who left their headlights burning & charge
exorbitantly for a jump. I admit sympathy

for teen-age girls dropped off by nervous
dads with baby sitting moola crammed in their

tiny pocketbooks. When I drink the stars appear
very impersonal so I know my twin exists

elsewhere & one of us knows the truth & has
conned the other into some sad isolation that

acts like a very disloyal yo-yo. If I think about it,
leaves cover trees less than half the year

but I think of the natural, sober state
of a tree as having leaves, not being bare.

The New World Deli

At a cocktail party I met the actual guy who cloned sheep.
The idea of replacement organs swirled in my strong

Drink, danced around a striped swizzle stick.
My mother died recently and I was curious about

Sharing some of her cells and having him bring her back
To life, but I had trouble finding a smooth segue

In the conversation. I know doctors hate to give free advice
At cocktail parties. Is splitting genes to create a new species

Better than bringing our loved ones back from the dead?
In most families the answer would have to be a fat yes.

At some point this guy will splice a human embryo
With, say, a giant redwood and it will grow into a man

Stationary for life but able to live for a thousand years,
Or a tree with legs, walking the streets in search of a good

Hash house that serves hotcakes with real maple syrup—
A kind of cannibalism, drinking the blood of its young,

Which at times ain't a bad idea. Imagine teen-age boys
With electric guitar picks for fingers, their left hands vaginas

Naturally, and everyone creating beings of their own choosing,
And no one ever dying unless they wanted to, and only unborn souls

Complaining at the human deli line, waving their fleshy numbers,
Screaming because they think they may have been skipped.

Secret Shoes

They have removed my shoe laces
Though I am not in jail nor is anyone
Afraid I might commit suicide.

Progressively I resemble an abstract child
Relearning to speak after the seizure in
A department store on the last shopping

Day. It is not part of the cashiers' job
Description to save my life. I am sleeping
On top of the blankets in a cheap motel

With my shoes laced & glasses still on.
I am just a boy coming home late &
My mother is waiting on the stoop;

I can tell even from this dusky distance
Her worry will turn to a slapping-screaming
Rage once she realizes I am safe. Funny

How emotions are quick change artists.
I count my hidden money several times
A day though not for miserly reasons.

My fingers are cramped & sore from
Writing in the margins of those
Mysterious standardized tests whose

scores are never shared with us.
My calluses are stained deep gray
From pencil lead. I have never written

What I actually thought & intend on
Doing so my entire life. My parents
Are having a cocktail party; most of

The guests are already tipsy, laughing
& gulping canned smoked oysters on
Tiny orange crackers. Everyone has piled

Their coats on the guest bed: mink stoles,
Long woolen overcoats, puffy imitation
Jackets. I climb on the heap & every one

Has a different odor, not all unpleasant.
When adults visit I become invisible
Which I like, especially when I crawl under

The dining room table & examine the ladies
Nylons & witness the men's wandering
Hands. I eavesdrop their conversations

Which should not be confused with the family
Secrets I should not repeat to anyone & all
Their beautiful complications that remain unlaced.

Law & Order

The coroner slices open her stomach & because the honeycomb
Tripe with parmesan has been only partially digested she
Deduces the victim was murdered less than an hour
After eating. Investigators focus on Italian restaurants

Within walking distance. Waiters are questioned
& shown a snapshot of the dead woman (more a girl really).
Of course it's possible she ate a home cooked meal
But because she drank an older *Carmignano Piaggia* with her

Uncommon dish detectives think it more logical to focus
On restaurants. You might think the body could have been
Dumped on the street so why focus only on local establishments?
Well, you have to start somewhere. You are born

At a particular moment & die at a particular moment.
The coroner detects cocaine & albuterol in the blood
So we know she is asthmatic & maybe a party girl.
She had had sex in the last hour of her life because

There is semen residue in her panties but DNA evidence
Reveals the intercourse occurred with two different men
Who happened to be in the same family. We find out the vic
Is the younger of two sisters but later learn that she is,

In fact, **not**, but the daughter of the older girl who has three
Distinct personalities, one of which is a thug named Hank.
There is a baby adopted from China who has a cancerous
Tumor time-bomb ticking in her brain that the adopted

Parents were not told about by the sleazy broker.
We are led to believe the baby was strangled by her autistic
Brother (also adopted) who had no history of violence.
The sad part is these folks would have taken the baby regardless.

There is a beautiful philanthropist who lures rich
Men into her spidery grasp & pries freshly written checks
Out of their white knuckles; she provides good charities with only
A miniscule portion. She profits, of course, from the exchange

& is also guilty of slipping a recreational Viagra Mickey
Into a politician's single malt scotch. He croaks from a heart attack
But is this murder? After all, she only wanted him to have the time
Of his life, unleash the secret body behind the beautifully dark side

Of the bricked up fireplace. There is the subtle evidence held back
Till the precise, most vulnerably effective moment. Confession is what
Makes us human. Maybe because our lives are so ordinary we are attracted
To those who peel off their skin, who don't mind deciding in an instant

Whether to take a deal & serve 10-20 or gamble on the sympathy
Of the jury, our fellow citizens. Pull the trigger darling, for me!
Happy to pass judgment, most of us have no stomach to
Witness the execution, nor serve time or even plan our own escape.

Exact Life-Time:

It'd be a very difficult world indeed if everyone had
a clock imbedded in his forehead: t-minus-x
till the afterlife, the public privy to precisely how many ticks
he has left on this pear-shaped planet, everyone but him!

Oh you should never ever tell anyone the truth, but he'd know.
By the treatment. Petty annoyances rarely worth bickering about,
he'd be likely to take unfathomable sexual risks with strangers.
He might not shave daily or watch his cholesterol but dance

beautifully on ripe bananas of futility. More on the bright
side: there'd be more unbridled sympathy & his embedded clock
could reflect personal style, antique numbers shaped like
avocados or whatever he'd like, whatever he'd like.

Small things would seem silly as they are. You might be
on the subway & bump into a passenger & know that by Friday
he'll be dead. That would affect you for a stop or two, wouldn't it?
Oh, you think it better these embedded clocks are presently invisible,

but all men could wear derbies over their eyes like Surrealists.
Women could wear veils. Men are forbidden to see their wives
faces & have to invent complicated signals only the two of them know
so they can recognize each other in the afterlife. That's real love.

You've seen old war movies. G.I.'s the night before they ship off
set their clocks ahead to convince their high school darlings to do it.
Problem is, once the clock's advanced, it can't be set back.
Young folks often make this mistake. Exact life-time could

make you so much more yourself, more apt to tell people what
you actually think. But imagine the worst sadness: holding your new
born & seeing she'll not live to her seventh birthday. You might
devote every waking second to her pure happiness & would this be

so terrible? But it's already terrible. You plan a trip to the Amusement
Park the week before the funeral, staying each night till the park closes,
till your feet are sore, till everyone is weepy from exhaustion,
& she has more stuffed animals than she can hold, her face a spider

web of cotton candy, & you hold your wife when your baby isn't
looking to hush her sobs or say how lucky you are that you know,
or how you wish you didn't, how the world was better in its absolute
uncertainty, or whatever you'd like, whatever you'd like.

Impending Hurricane

After we finally get the kids tucked in,
melt into the sofa, laugh tracks blaring,
begin wafting red table sludge from tumblers,

the Weather guy barges into our regular program—
Imagine a tornado of patio furniture! Stock up
folks on flashlights & bottled water, nail plywood to...

The storm swerves, of course, out to sea. On
Sunday we ponder like idiot savants the unexpected
sunshine, having canceled our cook-out. So much

ain't exactly as those with inside info predict.
I wish some Super Doppler hovered over our lives
to transmit intimate newscasts: footage of her moving

her lips after the phone is hung up, or the radar maps
that track how my testicles are knotted by amateurs.
In *our* esoteric hurricane, even well-rooted trees

exaggerate when gossiping & sway more than is wind
appropriate. I long for the days when weather was simple
as holding your palm to the sky. Most days I wear

coordinated clothes to the office & carry an umbrella in case.
When the most inventive & interesting brain storms occur
they never turn actual, like our phantom hurricane.

It happens I am tired of ordinary melodrama,
daily angst that nudges me off to work each damn day,
the methodical gravity that pulls my car towards home.

Mostly the shoulders of my pressed white shirts
are stained with baby vomit, but I do have infinite hands
& the tick-tocking of a random, linear clock.

As I was saying, I long for the days when weather was
simple as stepping onto the porch in just your pajamas
& looking up & blinking when a blade of rain gouges your eye.

Domestic Surrealism II

Every vacation drive smells like your arm hairs
singed from over dousing the briquettes

with aromatic lighter fluid, & lobbying for radio
control, & the kids cranky & spilling in the back seat—

Because so little is delectably dangerous anymore,
because women don't fold small notes into our hands,

we transparent men, hypnotized by too much
America, tailgate & honk at the slightest mistake.

Sometimes a random insult sucks you in, & you snap,
zapping off the radio. The guy who you cut off

shakes his fist & invites you & your pathetic
fallacy to pull over. Your wife inquires in her calm

if you are crazy, if you're aware he might have a gun,
which perks the kids up. *That jerk has a gun*, one says.

No you confess to your wife, you cannot articulate
the nature of your troubles, as though anyone could.

The guy pulls you out of the car by your shirt.
Some people are addicted to their own solipsistic

adrenaline so are habitually late. Others, when life
goes well, invent problems just to have a little focus.

It's hard to pinpoint precisely what ticks another human
off, & when the chaos of the fight swirls like cartoon tweeties

around your stupid head, what words can you retrieve which
might allow you to retain your dignity, the ability to tuck

your shirt back in, gracefully get back into the driver's seat?
After, you signal politely to inform the other motorists

of your noble intention to blend back into the traffic flow,
& you wave your swollen hand in thanks, invent a smile.

Little Bennie Against The World

I was the first grader in the Boy's room
who examined his receding hair line,
who gawked outside the ballroom window
of his Senior Prom & charted his mid-life crisis.
The girls I kissed that night were glass.

The problem of being: even with my foot
off the gas, my engine races at stop lights,
but my oily mechanic's diagnosis reveals
only mice nesting in the carburetor.
By the time tulips follow their intuition,

my odd collage of mice & gasoline will
collaborate with ghosts who exile
through tailpipes in heavy traffic.
Relish the flat sentence elevated by Godless
adjectives & solvent nouns, but ignore

the Truth: during a sneeze or orgasm
you can't keep your eyes open anyway.
Fret not, amigos. Really, no one belongs.
Nobody has good info. You learn to read
in first grade; the world expands then lies;

you learn to change your sparkplugs or
practice kissing your hand's hairy side.
Years later, you may be graced with actual love
& not find it paradoxical to want, to still want...
to replay comebacks you should've said.

You might even rip a sink from the wall.
Love's inadequacies begin to resemble rage...
but you haven't completely lost it yet,
even though the McDonald's drive-thru
attendant maliciously delays your burger.

So you lay a very heavy forehead on your horn
for a little eternity...
Or, something amazing could happen!
You may find breathing & breeding
from its own logic, something profound

& squeaking on the edge of understanding.
When you open your hood, pretending
the horn was malfunctioning, you discover
something like mouse fur in your engine,
which seems as close as you'd get to truth.

God in Pasta

Dozens of drivers claim
to have seen Jesus
in a billboard's steaming
bowl of spaghetti.

One young mother was leaving
her husband, at least skipping
choir practice, but divinely
compelled to look at the billboard,

and moved by the crown of thorns,
the sad, deep eyes squinting
rivulets of tomato sauce,
she slammed her brakes,

did a U-turn for home.
She'll keep her secret—
go back to all she never
confesses to him, utter faith:

plain boiling water
in a steel kettle after
the whole house is asleep.
An entire family so settled

into itself that even during
a power outage it
performs its rituals
without tripping over toys.

All the water's boiled
into vapor, the kettle white hot.
She lifts the handle without
thinking, without a pot holder.

Believers from one Italian village
walk on their knees for miles
over pebbles. Relatives encourage
them in rusty cars, windows down.

And her spaghetti stays brittle,
uncooked on the amazingly clean
counter, human in its rigidity,
its potential to soften, reshape.

Escaping God

When you shut your eyes to daydream, you're really
imagining the face of God, who, in the 50's, assumed
the face of Mrs. Oshkenozi, who sat in her apartment
window handing glasses of seltzer to boys
in pursuit of perfect stickball. Grandpa & his
compatriots puffed unfiltered Camels & flirted
with imperfect hands of gin, downing iced vodka
& pickled herring. Out of geographical ignorance
he invented a new ocean from Minsk
to a dank tailor shop on the lower East Side.

To this day, no male in my kin can decipher a road map.
My own father, for instance, circled the back roads
of Georgia three sweltering days past the same billboard
boasting giant alligators & the sweetest peaches,
wasting our one family vacation. Even to ask
directions violates the foundation of our religion.
Youth should bum around till their notions arrive.
The topic of my grandmother's voyage to America
was bananas, how she ate one, peel & all.
I can't erase the image, a beautiful Polish girl

in a coarse sepia dress vomiting over the rails,
praying to no God in particular.
I believe in everything so practice nothing,
thank Mrs. Oshkenozi, who became God in the Camps
& believed in nothing so practiced kindness.
A New Age Berkeley doctor convinced us circumcision
has no medical basis, so my boys, my mother scolded,
can't be buried in a Jewish cemetery because
they have more skin on their dicks than their ancestors.
Jewish men are eternal optimists, cutting off an inch

as soon as life begins. Once as a boy I heard a glass
drop from a window. "Mrs. Oshkenozi, is that you?"

"For once, she said, let's pretend it isn't to see what happens."
Clearly, she read too much Malamud, which reminds me,
I'm strangely proud grandpa was forced to read
in secret, that my father made no secret about not reading.
When he died, I was relieved I wouldn't have to be a Jew anymore.
My youngest son is my father reincarnated—perpetual scam
coated in human skin, a notion no one has come up with yet.
We're the only Jews in our town. My wife, who isn't,

is obliged each Winter to construct a little talk about the origins
of our faith to the elementary school. She brings the tops
& chocolate money, teaches a few songs. How everything
is based on a miracle, the comfort of not having to explain,
like any light burning longer than it should. In my house,
the unknowable generational beauty of each son
wearing his brother's hand-me-down pajamas—
redundancy becomes custom elevated to religion. Or just a mistake,
confusing one son for another, which is my concept of God.
Often, without thinking, I call him by the wrong name...

The Ghosts Of Luxury

Sometime in the 50's, Robert Frost, a visiting
professor at Berkeley, desired, Frost desired
to meet baseball players & was introduced
to a curly haired cherubic blond who later
became Rookie of the Year for the Bosox:
Jackie Jensen. They talked into the espresso
evenings mostly baseball but a little poetry too,

& stayed periodic New England pals.
Jackie often left tickets for Mr. Frost.
I'm embarrassed by my love for this story,
void of drama, its only point, the oddness of friends.
July, 1993, my first Fenway visit. The Green Monster.
Steel girders obstruct some of the cheap seats.
A man's value is measured by his seat at a baseball game.

I thought of my father, how he'd be a little proud—
me, in a sky box with free beer & unlimited franks.
The dead don't need to know the why of anything.
He'd just brag to his scalper cronies in heaven.
No doubt he'd think I've become something,
but what would he ask besides the names of my sons?
If I'm happy? I once swore I'd never

mention happiness in a poem, so I'd just nod.
I know loss & luxury began in 1961 because
the National League didn't exist, did not exist in New York.
I know it was 1961 because the city was buzzing
Mantle & Maris & 61 Jacks, the city pregnant
with Mets. Upon their birth in '62, my father
no longer needed to wake me at 4 a.m.

No, nothing was wrong. He simply needed to drive
to Philly to catch the Giants: the closest they'd get
to New York for a year. (Save the World Series).
In 1961, in the House That Ruth Built, my father

thought out loud. Look at those slobs in the bleachers.
If every one gave us a buck, no one would miss it,
or even think twice, & baby, we'd be fucking rich.

As time erodes, one's definition of luxury changes.
Any moron can identify the wealthy. Seasons
are so casual, so insignificant, they treat them as verbs.
(We summered along the Seine). At Fenway, my buddies
& I waited till everyone but the sweepers left the stadium,
then snuck onto the darkened field. Bob pretended to bat.
I threw an imaginary curve from the pitcher's rubber.

I believe I saw the ghost of Robert Frost in the bleachers—
Jackie Jensen in the dugout thumbing the complete
poems of the Queen of Amherst, & my old man,
wolfing a hot dog in three bites, a cigarette glowing
in his other hand. My definition of luxury is constant,
a baseball game, the way you plan nothing after
cause there's no telling how long it'll last,

the play not restricted by time, but by the number
of failures, (outs), a sport that invades all four seasons.
Luxury has changed. When I have a late work
meeting & not enough time to go home & come back,
I hoard the hour at a Chinese restaurant,
not thinking about my wife, the boys,
the third kicking her belly. After the meal,

the waitress formally announces: my fortune cookie.
I crumble it & find a lucky mistake:
three fortunes. I forget the first two.
The last said, *He who has imagination*
without the darkening has wings but no feet.
But even that may not be exactly right...
If not for failures, nothing would ever end.

Hitting A Skunk At 60 Miles Per Hour

I've been talking at night back to the car radio.
I've been talking back to the car radio at night,
coaching and coaxing mortality into a starry roadside diner
and witnessing my own intimacy hitchhiking
like an hysterical girl towards the highway.
I caressed jars of preserves and pickles in my cellar
but will not jinx my good fortune or taunt the spirits
by gloating over bins overflowing with rice, handsome sons.
I've heard the glass kiss of embryo pigs floating
in formaldehyde off the cellar shelf during an earthquake.

A Russian woman slurps coffee with two hands,
her hands warmed from the glass; her son plops
two black market sugar cubes into the milky ocean.
A hunter floats his permit into a nervous river.
Sleeping on hot-air vents in Oakland's China Town.
Paintings in blue-night and red-clay—
Pueblo pottery, Zuni, Papago, Yavasui, Apache.
Little League fathers slugging each other in bleachers.
Japanese yen spidering into the New York Stock Exchange.
Narcotic strains of THC exploding marijuana from secret forests
of Northern California. Rookie cops leaving their invisible
wives after making love to pump iron in the precinct.

Talking with the doctor to debate having our songs
circumcised...I mean our sons!
One out of four college girls is raped by someone known
and none of her friends refer to her by name
and wear their sunglasses even at night.
On modern machines that force us to run in place without
strain on joints and muscles, of virtual sex without touching,
from the great addiction to myth and much later,
from blowjobs in running cars to smokestacks in deserted
factories, rain forests shrinking and cities more resembling

jungles—women with war paint to buddy can you spare a sawbuck
panhandled by a man in dreadlocks so he can rent four videos.
Moving from minimalist black to country solid maple, snorting
Pure oxygen, from flapper logic and bathtub gin to reading to children—
Navajo blankets from the 19th century hawked in gas stations,
shown in museums of modern art. Highway gas station lavatories.
Leaking angels over a plate of steaming home fries in a diner.
We have been talking back to the night.
The Delta Blues indicate that your baby ain't sweet like mine
but damn it I want yours anyway. I want yours!

Dia De Los Muertos—because we are acquainted with death,
wear its skeletal masks in processions through the streets,
we can mock life, how every thing and not one thing matters—
how all is traced back to pleasure...
baking bread, washing a baby's back in the sink,
rolling up the car window on a hot summer night because
somebody ran over a skunk and flicked a lit cigarette
into the shut window, the fiery head fell onto the carpet
and can't be found, even if you could pull over and stop,
even if the aroma of smoke and skunk did not exist,
even if you could turn off the radio—and,
the moon in the corn swaying pasture is primitive as skin

against leaf. The light inside the refrigerator,
headlights left on, talking seriously to light bulbs as to God.
A man parachutes into a Hollywood wedding.
Sitting on luggage in airports, sitting on basketballs
in schoolyards, storing electrical appliances in cellars
with every good intention of fixing them.
Closets larger than rooms. A quick brushstroke
of ink which implies bamboo, a man guiding his father
over a stone bridge to taste first peaches,
a cup of glacier-water. Steady hand on an elbow.

Point A

Mostly it's finito, at least never the same,
after the first inebriation of breast milk.
So proceed: because that's all you can do.
What happens to you creates your philosophy.

If Adam invented Eve to be another sex,
to be inside someone else's body, isn't lust pure?
Man invented Adam because God's a hitchhiker
whose baseball cap shades his eyes...

It's so easy to understand mass murder, apartheid,
rape, the melting and hardening of inhuman wax,
but what about small difficult moments?
Think about any beginning. Before it discolors.

First stag party: one nude woman's shake
and shimmy on a table, red high heels,
vagina oozing whipped cream, one maraschino cherry.
Jeers are just cheap scotch in the shape

of guys you know. Guys you know.
Like a brown paper bag in the shape of a bottle.
Do you feel uncomfortable demeaning another?
To lick the air around someone's nakedness?

Then stop here. Get out of the car bitch.
Here's a dime. But the closest pay phone is nowhere.
That nude dancer comes from Nowhere.
No family, born with big jugs.

She invents even her own name: Cherry Cupcake.
You wonder what it would be like, not to be
with her (you know you'll get your dark chance some day),
but to stroll into a bar incognito,

gesture to the bartender with a smoky wink
and say Sloe Gin Fizz for the lady scotch rocks for me.
Towards midnight, you walk into the clammy drizzle,
your leather jacket over her shoulders...

So you impersonate art instead of life
and watch the Million Dollar Movie,
same movie three times a day for a week—
the dialogue becoming your attitude,

your tongue's grooves and goose bumps
you once thought were tonsils.
Greasers back their G.T.O.'s into Dutchess
and order from the skating waitress

cheeseburgers on a honeymoon, heavy mayo also.
Behind the dumpster, guys in drag mouth
Judy Garland lyrics. Friday nights St. Mary's
holds a dance; you pay two bucks to pretend

you're drunk, or, if you really are,
pretend to be sober.
This, too, is actual: an ex-girlfriend
from a zillion years ago sends a note

along with the list: you're one of the MIA's
from the 20-year high school reunion.
The note ends, love Lisa.
First girl you kissed. The note.

It makes you almost walk through a plate glass door.
But the middle sags—worn couch,
falling asleep to the TV, wakened by the blare
of the Star Spangled. You do love your country

at the ball park—the tingles
between bites of cold gray hot dogs.
Next memory, you old man's heart attack finale.
Your girlfriend calls from Sympatico, Mexico.

Mail the horse; I'll send the dough in a couple of days.
The selfish lying cheating scams stop
and you arrive at Point B:
regular job, civil letters to the IRS,

tipping the paper boy instead of
pounding the vending machine for freebies.
Then, your landlord Ilene informs you
a political refugee from Latin America

will be bunking in your rented basement;
what she doesn't say is he'll sponge
your electricity, his Mickey D wrappers
will attract rats, his black and white tube

will blast at all hours, Spanish stations.
Across town, young couples nibble arugula salads,
slurp raw Blue Points, sip Chateau Suideraut, 1983.
All sensuality. Conversation seeps like breast milk.

Will compassion in America ever be brought up
from the minors? Your landlord left her husband
to live with her lover—two stocky women
holding a wobbly ladder for each other.

You think of sleeping with two women at once.
Adam started by counting his ribs.
You negotiate a rent decrease.
Very adult. No vulgarities.

Domestic Surrealism

When I'm lonely, I ride the train into the city.
When I take a train into the city I feel lonely

so drive, articulated by traffic, its flow, breathing
in, not letting out, a normal guy with his windows

rolled up, doing my time in a human sentence,
starched shirt, tortured by paper cuts

on my tongue from sexually licking bill envelopes,
& it comforts & frightens me that each frenetic soul

is the product of two people making love,
even in this city of millions of squeaking beds,

slippery gambles, not even well groomed shadows
of my father who was reduced to a name sewn

on a denim shirt above his right pocket, opposite his heart.
Lava flooded his dry cleaning business—

Head down against an unemployed wind, pausing,
petrified by his reflection in display windows

where faceless mannequins dress flimsily for summer,
stiff women he'd never meet, in a season that never

actually arrives, he must have confronted his personal Pompeii.
I'm still a boy who slams his bicycle flat, too rushed

for a kick stand, the back wheel spinning till it slows
so majestically I can see the spokes, like women

without make-up. I love women beyond comprehension
& want to comprehend women beyond lust.

That's why I small talk to the recently divorced,
the pretty voice of the phone solicitor who interrupts

dinner, trying to entice me into a Platinum credit card.
I ask always for her home number but not one

to date has relinquished her precious digits.
I know the answer though: some random string of 1

through 9, but a fat zero could be thrown into the mix.
What we don't know is the order. The secret's the order.

That's what separates us from each other,
our swirling DNA like a new hairdo in wind.

My lust's evolved so it no longer depends upon
getting into her pants; it's the challenge to talk

her out of the black panties of her soul.
You can't blame me although I know you must.

Precious digits. Unlisted phone numbers.
Personal DNA strands that make our children

resemble us. Really, all we want are diversions—
fathering children to see how the harm done

is no different from any boy secretly playing with dolls.
Or some other game, where we accumulate extra lives.

The Salvador Dali Exhibit: Rome, 1999

Rarely have you had a crush on a word so surprisingly instrumental
You are reminded how yielding the world can be. In a café in Rome
You are introduced to *limoncello*, take an experimental sip & think,

Yes, sometimes a word can be so sensual it veers off its main road
Of abstraction. Mussolini resurfaced less popular ruins with sleek
Streets but present citizens thought better of it. You took a stroll

In the blazing Roman afternoon to get a closer peek at the lackadaisical
Archeology, the heavy machinery & delicate brushes, the official
Looking women with notepads & deep tans, & softly cruel

Expressions, but were sidetracked by a Dali exhibit. In his pastel
Illustrations of Dante's Cantos, God never appeared, never appeared so
Vibrant, so much as such a dreamy explosion of communist machine

Gun fire & *limoncello* drooping over a terrace garden as a not yet
Realized form. Each time citizens begin excavating the Roman streets
For a subway they bump into another layer of undiscovered ruins.

At some point, your wife says, they should get on with their modern
Lives. Isn't contemporary traffic worse than being unaware of your past?
Like Dali's depiction of the Tree of Sorrow, as if leaves were an exclusive

Alphabet whose shadows camouflage the tree itself. You'd been having
A hard time with your wife & there was a Dali sofa in the shape of luscious,
Red lips, *limoncello* lips & a little sign that instructed you to not sit on it.

Outside is a blueness of not yet dark but the streetlights waffle. Shoes
Are popular with tourists & you love the instrumental clicking of good
Leather soles on the cobbled streets. Each narrow lane's a lazy dream,

From each high window, a woman hanging laundry & a poster of Dali
Proclaiming "I am not mad!" You'd have to admit, at this point, your
Acceptance into heaven is borderline at best. All women are thin of course

With dark, skintight, sleeveless shirts. In the crowded market, a nursing
Mother throws her baby at you! As you reach to catch it, (it turns out to be
Newspapers wrapped in a blanket), a little army of urchins pick

Your very disloyal pocket. Your dollars magically convert to lire.
For that instant you see Christian art in the asymmetrical
Weathered daily faces. Are you suspicious of all the wrong things?

Is a man defined by his worst or best moments? Is Dali's waxed
Moustache testament to the fact that the only abstract painting is monogamy?
There's something to be said about covering the past with fresh, modern roads.

Obsolete Organs

The Lord hasn't kept very current.
Even some body parts are obsolete.

No one alive remembers the appendix's purpose.
Often during major surgery doctors will remove

The gall bladder if it looks funny or is riddled
With stones. No big deal. We live fine without

Some of which we were born with. But
I worry our hearts might drift out of fashion.

Already there is a serious lack of compassion:
Beheadings on the internet, children rummaging

Through garbage, nuclear families separated
By tidal waves. It's a cliché that hardly anyone

Looks into the eyes of a panhandler but if he
Could auction his kidney to your dying kid...

I was in a rush for the babies to walk
But now when they ask for the car keys I wish

I could squelch the hormones of linear time.
Some surgeries your heart actually stops;

In some surgeries they pop your eyes balls out
Then put them back. We have evolved where

Even the process of reattaching a finger depends
Upon wrapping it in a clean ice filled cloth

& speeding to the hospital because God hasn't
Kept current by allowing us to re-grow body parts.

If Every Man Were A Robert De Niro

I worship as my Lord the confused & convoluted
contusions of late afternoon light—
the guy who at dawn builds a pyramid
of champagne glasses & sips from each one—
the construction worker who hurls his plate
of meat loaf & ketchuppy spuds against a wall.
I'm the only breathing guy at this weekday matinee.

Popcorn's not even warm.
The usher doesn't bother to tear my stub.
A drunk in the *Ladies Room* dolls up by painting
a lipstick smile beyond the borders of her lips.
Makes her clowny, the lavatory light.
I see someone's lost wallet on the velvet seat

I'm about to sit in so change rows.
The drunk, now sober on theater darkness,
which I worship as my Lord, sits in the balcony.
My desire travels the illegal borders of lipstick,
like "Coyotes" smuggling migrant grape pickers
over the desert at dusk,

like a womanless man buying lipstick at a drug store,
like the one kiss that propels you through this life.
On the way home, meander at a magazine rack
thumbing what I'd never buy. I know the days & hours
only by particular TV shows. You think I'm pathetic?
You ask how the days defeat their own purposes?
Here's my motto: Praise the quick glance.

Life's desire. You know what I mean. Maybe you don't.
Let's start from this lonely dot. I'm walking home
from a movie about the way two strangers sip
the coffee of each other's alien sensibilities
& wind up in the sack. You pace yourself a step
behind & I smell the warm bakery rolls

with poppy seeds you're carrying in a brown paper bag.
I can't name your perfume (or any) but there's
a hint of citrus. I can tell by the sound
of your steps you're not used to walking
in high heels. I could be some loony who whips
out one of those pug nose revolvers. But I turn

& say I can't decide if you or the rolls smell better.
You pretend to ignore me & I feel like a cardboard
De Niro, TV left blasting in my studio apartment,
lights off. Sometimes I phone myself to see if
I'm home. The traffic signal says DON'T WALK
but you trot the way women do in high heels,
women who have someone improbable to get to.

The Missing Thirteen

I plant red flowering Bee Balm to attract hummingbirds
then hummingbirds loiter & dart in my garden.

I make love to my wife & immaculately she is pregnant!
I'm continually surprised when the diagram is actualized.

I've been reading the jazzy unrevised final poems
of the John Berryman who microscoped his encored

humiliations in the Pre-Betty-Ford booze treatment
factory, surrendering an isolated tear of an unpronounceable

sedative into a sequence of liquid syllables so suspended
they could not be scanned. Mr. Berryman, I tip my invisible

cap to your tottering music, recognize your unshaved mug
in the hung-over bees in my garden, & I stop

for the collective Summer stare of a family
on the highway's soft shoulder beside their station wagon,

the hood open & steaming, a rear tire flat. They unload
their suitcases & vacation loot from the trunk just to get

at the jack & spare, which, as you guess sir, is also deflated.
In the last thirty minutes the wife has started to show.

The father of this mess hot-foots it to the nearest Texaco.
I'm never surprised by the never-coming-back, the unexpected

cloudburst. Mr. Berryman, kids still goose-step in the center
of puddles, unmarried women, dolled up, delicately avoid them,

& everyone, splashed by a joy ridden car of newly licensed
teens, has an affair with evaporation. Don't you love

how water is chameleon? How its presence or absence influences
the inky newsprint of our dailiness: a baseball rain delay,

famine in Zaire, the discovery of rivers on Mars?
If I believed in God, she would be exclusively water,

not like us, only 87 percent. Because of the missing 13,
we discreetly attach ourselves to our desires

like a girl at a party who places her hooks
in an older boy with a car. Mr. Berryman, bad news:

the traditional notion of reincarnation is obsolete.
You ain't comin' back. Other news is also not good.

Since your exodus, most have converted to the metamorphosis
of water: Liquid entices Gas to a party but leaves with Solid.

You know the words to that song. You hum & tap your feet.
A great-great somebody dies & during the holiday

from human form, his spirit multiplies. This explains
why we think we know someone just introduced, how sometimes

we absolutely trust strangers: we once were the same
person. As when you saw your staggering reflection

in the river below the bridge & were surprised
by the watery diagram of your face, your face hovering

like a hummingbird before darting off to its mysterious
infidelities. That water must keep you distant from God.

Cherries Out Of Season

We love to assign names to simplify life: this is my agent,
Or let me introduce you to my wife. Relationships hover
Outside our curious definitions. There is a peak season
For cherries, but sometimes in winter, a stray, expensive
Bag will infiltrate the grocery, exiled or deported from Latin
America. They never taste the way you would expect or hope.

Pop a dark one into your mouth but don't spit the pit until you
Reach the snack aisle & go undetected. The concept of deception
Is not being disloyal to your ideals: when I have zero dollars
I do not necessarily have nada. Oftentimes when I have nothing
I am flush with folding money. I am sitting in a parked car; it is
Raining & the motor is running & I should flip on the defroster

Because my windshield is fogging but you are talking, trying to
Define what it is we are. The haze between being enlightened
& duped is a border crossing in a metaphorical Brazil & you shove
Your forged passport in the face of the guard who confiscates it.
It is not you. At least it doesn't look like you. But that was years
Ago you plead. Your hair had not yet turned grey. You were ripe.

Pockets

Once after the evening news
my grandmother teased her hair,
a beehive, then began sewing
our pockets shut,
every garment in the house.

A pocket is the most perfect illusion.
I didn't know what illusion meant
but it sounded like a beautiful shame,
a woman in a white dress losing
her balance along a Polish riverbed.

When I woke at five a.m.
to deliver the morning edition
she was still at it.
Everybody already awake.
My father said she was dead

but she was sewing pockets shut.
My father worked at the mint
printing money in pocketless jumpsuits
so he couldn't take any home—
so what could he know about death?

They didn't want me at the funeral.
My father did though so I went.
I brought a needle and thread.
She came back to life for a second.
Even my father said it happened.

When my father tried to talk he wanted
to put his hands deeply into the pockets
of his good black pants, but they,
of course, were sewn shut.
He seemed to want to confess

the private about his mother.
How she escaped from Poland.
The way she drank sugary coffee
in a clear glass with two hands.
The mysterious way she sewed in the dark.

Clean

We came home cranky from a long winter drive,
freezing stiletto rain pecking our windshield.

Just off the highway Jake drifted to sleep
but woke when lifted from his car seat.

He whined for a hot bath—the phone message
machine blinking—the house stumbling dark—

thinking we'd be home before dark.
I ran his bath, helped him out of his clothes.

One shoe had fallen off in the car. He eased in,
whispering, *perfecto*, then lay there, not thinking,

lost in shallow water, counting faucet drips;
I read a hard cover on the icy linoleum.

Still grumpy from the drive, Leslie flopped upstairs—
her home pregnancy test that morning the *big fat yes*.

I snapped Sam into his dryer-warm P.J.'s, commenced
to fry some eggs. Twin yolks from their brown shell

sizzled in hot butter. My wife believes, I don't,
in premonitions—so I tossed the double yolk,

wiped the black frying pan clean.
Let's just say I've been on a low cholesterol diet.

Before living with wife and sons, I devoured Fridays
the "all-you-can-eat" at The King's Table

after a week of steam cleaning carpets, then lugged
my own laundry in a mesh bag down Palo Verde. Ave.

to the Cactus Laundry Mat. After a man's clothes
are washed he becomes the most tragic of creatures,

just a guy with an armload of soggy towels
hovering by the spinning dryers, waiting his turn.

My father, a lifer in the dry cleaning biz,
was flush particular days rifling through strangers'

pockets. This is legal. It was his place.
Private riches from private pants in public space.

I wash my face in the bathroom mirror muttering, *father
of three, father of three.* No matter how hard I scrub

the face is still there. Jake's fingers, withered
into bath raisins, change channels. Outside, snow

confronts its existential collapse in streetlights
as I reach to erase the answering machine before we listen...

Hidden Costs

Some terrible mornings, the gravitational force
Within his coffee is sour milk. (He drinks it anyway).
He checks the empty mailbox barefoot quick over rocksalt
icy asphalt. The newspaper still in orbit.
If his universe lost fifteen pounds it'd be perfect.

He loves the incognito of hotel restaurants: nobody knows
his little history & he orders drinks esoterically:
Pinch on the rocks, but don't pour the scotch
over the ice! He really can't have another—
He's gotta be up early, drop the car off & hoof it to work.

Mechanics, you know, always find something.
It's never just an oil change. That's why he signs a form
authorizing them, in essence, to arbitrarily fuck him:
he even leaves a number where he can be reached.
No wonder when his life makes strange rattling

noises he ignores them & hopes they just go away.
No wonder he doesn't wanna talk. His wife says
"it's a small problem, just a little thing,"
but hidden behind the why do you leave dirty socks
on the wet bathroom floor is the "What's wrong with me?

How can you walk out just when the kids are through
college, the house nearly paid off?" Wedged in
each conversation is the real talk, as the greater
beauty eclipses the lesser one. When he picked up his wife
for their first date, emerging from the upstairs shadows

with wet hair, intentionally loosening her towel,
the more delicate sister. After a bedroom door slams,
the real trouble begins. Even routine documents
are part of the conspiracy. Try deciphering the mechanic's
bill: the camouflaged costs between parts & labor.

Between the beautiful futility of parked cars, he won't cross:
traffic hides itself. The hatcheck girl, in her closet of furs,
smiles as she hands him his number, later, her hand in his
pockets. Maybe because he'll be eating alone, she gives
the extra smile. The waitress tonight is especially chatty,

but the guy says: "Just don't ask me any questions!"
She's knocked for a loop but inquires should she just
bring the menu. He's fuming now & repeats: "I said
just don't ask me any damn questions. Can you do that?"

The Whispering Campaign

Hazy Friday afternoon, traffic slugs.
I get off a strange exit, miles before mine,
hoping for the short cut home. Between tenements,
the sun's intuition peeks through a pink
bowling shirt on a clothesline.

I project the night. After a shower,
my evening peck—the clink of glasses—
kids' muted voices of cocktail hour—
I never glue any more photographs in the album:
instead: stash my family in ice cube trays.

I'm lost. Literally. I just want back
on the congested highway. A male = reluctant
to ask directions, I orbit. No one anymore
speaks English anyway I say to myself.
The things one never says out loud...

Eavesdropping phone operators?
At coffee breaks they swap gossip,
play the intimate tapes, tap codes on the trafficky
wires that electrocute pigeons during thunderstorms.
The thing one never utters

is we're all quickies. Eternal Life's a con
to keep us in check. Listen, chaos would have too much
kick without sugar and milk. The kettle might whistle
itself blue-dry. I find the freeway by luck.
A fantasy: what if every car simultaneously runs out of gas?

All the crazed drivers slam doors
of stalled vehicles mumbling *What the fuck?*
Even passengers get a little nervous.
And so begins the whispering campaign.
Commuters, who otherwise change lanes without signals,

make delicate joint decisions: whether to hike for help
or remain with their cars, a polite chaos
because the world has lost its ability to move.
Those with phones are paranoid
and choose not to call, at least anyone they know.

Good people, though strangers,
start kissing and screwing on the still hot hoods.
This stalled religion of amoral traffic,
where even operators know as little as we,
permits us to say out loud what we usually whisper.

A song on the radio brings me back in the nick
to be tempted to violate the yellow and black
detour posted on my exit ramp.
But I'm a lawful citizen.
I drive beyond where I live.

Voyeur Voyager

I had worn this parasitically invisible suit since
August & took miniscule bites from lemons I
Smuggled in each pocket so I wouldn't come down
With scurvy. I had not had a conversation all
Autumn that did not resemble a curse or chain mail.
I came to a spiritual epiphany with the doctrine
That I am ugly but have not always been so.
My face has only violated its molecular treaty.

I am very American now which means it is more
Likely I'll die without my gallbladder & I drift
In the night towards jazz, naming the stars'
Illegitimate children. The monotonous days fill
With color the way a mouth fills with blood after
An unexpected punch. It's nothing personal; the world
Is nothing personal; it just wants to pretend to belong.
I recognize how few people I like & who talk to me.

Each morning I watch the ferry import my neighbors
To the city to their boring jobs & wish I was one
Of them. Often I walk past their apartments at night.
Table lamps are too bright of course. I see the wife
Setting the table & children horsing around.
Some even seem to be helping. Sometimes I can
Smell the pumpernickel or see a few wisps rise
From casseroles. I have no idea what I'm doing.

I walked into a department store & hundreds
Of televisions were tuned to the same movie.
All those TVs & just one sluggish story, but
The color was not exactly the same in any two.
I have a neighbor who hates human intimacy
So he married his television after a rocky courtship.
He confesses to it & sometimes allows it
To speak long after he has gone to bed.

Dressing In The Dark

If I were human I would be one who never
Wishes to go to sleep & never wants to wake
Up. If I were a cedar I would want to be cut

Down by two naked women, no chain
Saw, just the synchronized, methodical thwack
Of identical alternating exquisitely sharp axes.

Then I could be snow, the wet, heavy kind
Everyone hates to shovel, that freezes over
Night after it's become gravel-filthy. I would

Be the mysterious footprints discovered next
Morning. If I were an abandoned room I would
Boast a dozen coats of paint, all different

Colors, from egg shell to pathetic rose,
The deepest layers laced with lead. I would be
A novel that was so moving the reader

Would not dog ear a single page. If I were
A man I would dress in the dark rather than
Wake my wife. Dressing in the dark could be

Construed as sneaky, but what is more
Considerate than letting the person you love sleep,
Than letting the person you love never go to sleep.

Domestic Surrealism: The Late Guests

rattled from traffic & zombied from the prognosis, & me:
pacing, crushing cocktail ice between my gold fillings,
the molecules of the minutes tick & mutate.

It's standard sports fans: radiation, chemo, then surgery
to remove the lymph node & part of Lon's tongue so he might
not be able to talk or eat properly, which would damper

future dinner parties. The body is often an inhospitable host,
but I offer Deb extra aspirin for the way she migrained
from the appointment, her head out the passenger window,

detached from her body, glasses off, & the radio on but
unhearable. Unbearable? Anyone settling into some new
terrible news slow motions his past indiscretions

from all sides so his private life may seem to contradict
his visible one. Haven't you ever witnessed a sun shower,
raining on only one side of the street? It's a Picasso thing—

too many mouths— too many questions—& all on one side
of his face. Here in summer, we often neglect to close, let alone,
lock the doors. In a city you're afraid of what could crawl in.

In the hubbub of pouring drinks our baby called 911 to report
my neglect to play a round of Go Fish. His brother,
not clear which one, coaxed him. When the squad cars

pulled up he fumbled in his mind to invent little alibis
that could safely carry him from this blue uniformed world
to the glorious inconsequential one inside him where his cells

remain motionless, nobody here but us chickens. He takes
after me: on business in the big city I random some name
from the phone book. Dial. But it seems to ring forever.

At this point I charade polite questions about the treatment
& switch the talk to sports & a newly planted garden.
Funny, tumors in conversation don't ruin anyone's appetite.

I suppose you only need to put off cancer till you have time
to die from something else, & then put that thing off, etc...
Really, it's courageous & life affirming, but what else can you do?

Pranks & College Literature

This girl in my Math class, a young woman,
pities me, though not enough to let me slide
my hand down her jeans, invites me to tag along
to a bash where she believes she biblically
hath known the host. Between shots of tequila
& bites of lemon I rummage his medicine cabinet.
A little traveling music baby, extra darkness please.
So without her I drive home, my headlights
off & eyes sealed till somebody honks.
I pull up to a toll booth, palm the attendant
an extra four bits & say I wish to pay
for my buddy in that rusty Chevy two cars back.
To glimpse his benefactor's license plate
the puzzled driver zooms, but I'm floored &
change lanes like whatever philosophy I'm reading.

There's a million schemes to make a buck—
hawking Kafka T-shirts at a neo-Nazi rally—
but it's tough thinking up ways to give one
away & make the recipient buggy to boot.
With my lower case ethics, I run a red light,
3 a.m. Is this still, on a deserted street,
a crime? Brush up, doll face, on your Zen.
I've learned to destroy worlds on postage
stamps with one unthinking lick, to hijack
plastic cow heads from idle milk trucks &
swipe peopleless suitcases in train stations—
& the pragmatic moon follows the connect-the-number
penumbra handcuffed to her id. Vacantly I remember
a story about Chekov & an ashtray. The ashtray
flies across the room, the smoke curling in the shape...

Most things that fly across the room resemble birds.

Home Town Chemistry

In a posh New York café, a bottle of mineral
water is served, infested with mutant bacteria
from secret underground tests in the Southwest.

Oh microscopic Government & her invisible uniforms.
I visited St. George Utah once where each
medicated citizen was scabby with skin cancer.

What I do with my hands in my pockets
is my own damn business thankyouverymuch.
I can change into anyone: I stash cash in my shoes.

Darn germs make me say things I don't mean.
Only taxes turn me inside out.
I dial continually 911 or the sweet prefix, 976.

Pursue the genuine by flipping channels.
Those who subsist on subway scams,
Pick pocketing & panhandling & slowly unbuttoning

their overcoats, Pandoraing if you will,
I tell them, wanna kill me? Then kill me.
It don't matter—this tape will self-destruct

in twenty seconds, or thirty years.
Are you spooked when a homeless reveals
his perversions as you rustle some coins

so Grand Canyon deep from your pockets?
If you value nothing you have everything, right?
In a rearview mirror on a Yuma Arizona

highway during a monsoon, I saw a mirage:
Hopi kids pinballing between Jumping Cholla
& Prickly Pear, rain dancing with dust devils.

Hypnotized by broken white lines & radiolessness
I braked then climbed the rocky ledge at Gilbert's Pass
& witnessed actual rain immigrating from Mexico

like a nimbus of illegal aliens transformed
into killer bees, absorbing our final oxygen.
Take a deep breath. See. Even now it's hard to breathe.

Though I've bargained for blankets in Nogales
& scalded my tongue on endangered turtle soup
lately I mostly watch & drool in sleep. Only

watch TV with the sound off. In the desert sometimes
bolts of lightning have second thoughts.
The wind interrogates Russian Thistle:

code name: Tumbleweed. Not native,
incidentally, to America. Stowaway seeds hoboed
in trouser cuffs of immigrants who were themselves

seeds, & popped up in the wild wild west
as mobile plants. Rootless. Flourishing.
& the bitter peyote irony: us city folks

can't leave our birth town without dying
too early from strangeness. If you remember,
at the bottom of Pandora's box, after each

molecule of Evil had escaped, Hope remained.
A further twist: we can't comprehend God the way
plants are baffled by our walking without roots.

Neighborly Love

I never imagined modern barriers—
mortgage payment, driving the horde
to piano lessons or Tai Chi,
my friends' cliché stories of divorce

would define me, slouching with guys
at bars & blackjack & bleakness.
So my favorite season is the movies—
clear morality, black & white redemptive tales—

(only the Found are comfortable with ambiguity)
as long as the theater is air-conditioned.
So my rage only emerges left foot first
into daylight after an afternoon matinee when

driving home, some unknown cuts me off
& I point a finger and curse him with
a miserable life, mild accident,
only moderate injury. A family man,

my ruthlessness is temperate.
Though my emptiness is caused by a lack
of courage to embrace any one belief,
combined with my sincere love of sport on cable,

an utter lack of compassion for the anonymous,
the faceless whose shopping cart I steal from
under the fluorescent lights into my own cart.
I love burgers but would be reluctant to hunt.

After decades of pick-up basketball games,
I witnessed its most violent conversation—
arguments are the norm, vulgarity, cheating,
unbridled fairness, but two guys maliciously

hacking, taunting after each bucket...
& after the game the trash continued.
"You don't know anything about me—all you know
is my name is Larry—I could be a murderer...

a mass murderer." The other guy said he'd already,
in fact, killed someone—so not to fuck with him.
Sometimes the finger I point at the rude motorist
makes the sound of an Uzi which sprays

saliva through my lips. A wife scans her husband's
computer files & discovers he's been cheating
on her—throws him out, ah, technology!
This is the story a friend tells me from his dim,

rented room. How he got caught. But now that
he has, he's glad. What life was it anyway?
I was looking through him, thinking of the game
I was missing on TV, filled with angst

over not programming my VCR.
The desire to will misfortune on someone's life
who's wronged us, or worse,
to be disinterested in a friend's grief evokes

a constant drizzle, a boom-a-rang curse,
like your name drawn in a heart on the sidewalk
beside a name you don't recognize,
though the writing is yours, though your name

is methodically being erased by a pounding
basketball. I've always worshipped good intention
too much—anonymous neighbors who battle,
with water buckets from hand to hand,

to douse a barn fire, children chasing hysterical horses.
Next morning, amidst the dawn & wisps of smoke,
they begin laying foundation for a new barn.
I thought of this movie scene on my new lawn.

In real life, the next door neighbor doesn't
wave when we're both raking leaves. The man
across the street sold his house after 16 years.
Only in the neighborhood a week, I offered to help

him move. I wanted to be one of the neighbors
but I was the only one. How could a man live
in a house for 16 years & not have friends
who'd help him lift heavy objects into a rented truck?

Last night in the city, a drive-by shooting
left a pregnant mother of two bleeding on the sidewalk.
The chalk outline of her body the police sketched,
after the crowd dispersed, simply dissolved in the rain...

Spring Baseball

Pine trees envy
the wind's liberties

so sway sometimes
on a still day.

A small boy wears his
brother's baseball cap.

The Catch

Summer's dusk, my father escorts his body home, dry cleaning slung over his shoulder, a crooked smile. A mild breeze slaps its own stubble face like baseball cards clothes-pinned to a boy's bicycle spokes as he escapes into another place. And I'm waiting for my Pop on our cement stoop, tossing a ball repeatedly into the air, an autographed ball that must never touch the ground...

All night my oil-soaked Felipe Alou model glove lay under my bed, arthritically gripped around a ball, tied with kite string, forming a pocket so perfect it would seduce the ball from the air, a sexy principle of physics.

The world delays for just us to play catch before dinner.

Then it's too dark to see, but we throw the ball high in the moonlight a few times anyway and catch it each time.

There are infinite beauties laced with hope that entice us to constantly reinvent our lives. Baseball is a solitary game, not nine men, but one boy pitching against a brick wall under a streetlight: the batter's shadow outlined in chalk, his sweet zone a different color.

And roaming the emerald outfield of the boy's imagination, over the freshly cut grass and freshly watered dirt, nine heroic faces, sons to sorrow and victory, spit tobacco juice, punch the pockets of their gloves, tap their muddy cleats with the bat handle before stepping into the lime outline, poised and frightened as though privy to some biblical secret or unexpected future, the way a good outfielder can sometimes sense the ball's flight and speed even before the batter swings, how he looks to the sky and sees, for an instant, nothing spiritual or human, only clouds and expansive blue, and the world is neither father nor son to anything, but just the impatient seconds waiting for the ball to return to earth that tempt us to be ruthless and loving enough to catch it cleanly...

Crybaby Blues

I woke up this morning & my teen-age son strums
His electric Fender with a Crybaby wah-wah pedal.
He's into feedback, Pretty Mama, & not the kind
For self-improvement. My kids are growing facial hair
& quick flipping the channels when I walk into the room.
I woke up this morning & the hound dog wind

Blew the trash can top down the street & I was
Rolling & tumbling after it in my boxers. Raccoons
Got into our garbage & ripped up the plastic bag
Leaving lamb bones & a used tampon on the lawn.
My car needs a jump. My heart needs a jump.
I woke up this morning & the shower was like ice.

There are no buttons on my coat, pretty baby, & my socks
Have holes & the mailman uses a battering ram to shove
The bills into my mailbox. I woke up this morning
My baby was gone. I think she must have gone on her jog.
I smelled bacon frying & coffee percolating & I was
Sweating in my bathroom mirror, my razor hand shaking

& everybody late for something & blaming each other.
I woke up this morning & gave my children an evil eye.
I opened the drawer & took out their voodoo dolls
& rusty pins & put a hoodoo in their lunch boxes.
My heart needs a jump. My heart needs a jump. I say
Don't be a baby, baby, & let the baby have his bottle.

Math

Clouds divide evenly into prime numbers.
Children are warned to avoid adding

faces & masks, but why?
The world's guilty of combining the oddest.

I've seen a woman apply fingernail polish,
not her shade, at her husband's funeral.

I've savored twenty-year-old Bordeaux
with Cheese Whiz on Ritz.

I've gone to work with a horrid fever
& called in sick for no reason.

Some people purchase life insurance on their kids.
Windows also reflect.

One requires dry wood most when it's raining.
I dance only when nobody is my partner.

The planets circle the sun nightly
the way a slightly drunk husband

circles his block for an hour
before he pulls into his driveway.

Headlights left on—
so God conceals His mistress.

So we have prime numbers
& the sky is continuous.

Cocktail Tree

I walk guilty through the airport's metal detector. As we buckle into our cramped seats, an Asian man with an un-tucked shirt whispers to the muscular blond steward, "Could you help me lift my bag into the overhead?" "Come on. Give it a try!" prodded the steward. "I can't; I have Polio in my right arm." I pictured a small courtyard in Arizona, the afternoon citrus light, and the concept of a cocktail tree, grafted at root and trunk, half grapefruit and half lemon, and wondered about combining humans the way magazines have us combine the features of the sexiest women to make one perfect specimen who is neither desirable nor interesting but who fulfills every desire. Or how angels long for human ambiguity and count us lucky for not seeing the absolute in things. Insurance baffles them.

I was sitting in a lounge with my wife and her sister reading magazines and sipping vodka and grapefruit juice in the shade of that cocktail tree. It's supposed to be warm, even at Christmas. Colored lights twisted around cacti, tipsy Santa in shorts and sunglasses waving from the roof, and, in the cool dusk, brown paper lunch bags weighted with sand are lit with candles: luminarias tracing the walkways of stucco houses. On the plane Leslie was breastfeeding Sam so his ears wouldn't clog and the Asian man read a popular novel and glanced at her exposed breast. Jake was mystified how he turned the page with the back of his withered hand.

Peculiar custom, both my sons were named before birth, labeling something before you know what it is. So many of us are walking around with names that don't fit. Or maybe we grow into and out of our names like a father's sweater. They shape us as we are sometimes shaped by others' conversations.

I know Leslie and I squabbled during the week in Arizona and her sister became upset and started to tear. She huffed into her old room with the almost empty glass of ice and focused on the black flask in her suitcase. In the wake of bitchy silence, Leslie and I did not recognize ourselves and recognized ourselves too damn well.

Night sat down to dinner. The wine was sour and we groped for terminology to describe the nuances of flavor that might justify the undesirable aftertaste in our mouths. Adult children in their childhood house comparing grapefruits and lemons just because they grew from the same tree; the orange branches withered after only one season.

Epilogue:

We are pleased, Mr. Fill-in, to accept your suicide note
But because of a terrible, terrible backlog & lack
Of University funding will not be able to publish it

Until the winter issue & only if your life doesn't improve.
Fortunately my self esteem, or, as my wife's student wrote,
Self of steam, is not tied into an external world validation.

I'm more of an internal lottery type of guy. Knowing that
The world is, & I apologize for my cultural insensitivity,
An Indian Giver, I try to remain disengaged. "Drinking

& gambling, staying out all night, living in a fool's
Paradise." Henceforth, I get my best ideas for poems standing
Over a urinal, eking out the last few drops before the little shake.

Others' inspiration comes in different places I suppose.
The most perfect invention is the oscillating fan. Notice
How I leap to a seemingly unrelated idea slash image.

Watch how I manipulatively tie it back to the initiating
Material & now that you're expecting it, I won't.
Keep your eye on the slight of hand & the narrative shift.

You don't require validation from the external world either so
You're a groom who doesn't show up for his own wedding.
Your wife to be hyperventilates into a paper bag, atoms of

Impatience speed up the tapping shoes of the most skeptical
Guests, their soles sticky with a bubble gum of revenge,
Designer food going cold, champagne losing its bubbles.

The hired help lean against a wall, thinking about their own
Unbearable lives, the ordinary errands after their shift ends.
So the poem gets mundanely complicated. The best images only

Verge on clear meaning, but encourage you to read on, like
A promising day that pushes you off the plane without a parachute,
& the swirling scenery seems so surreal you reconsider.

Acknowledgements

All the poems from this collection, sometimes in altered forms, originally appeared in the following periodicals. Grateful acknowledgement is made to the editors of these magazines for their receptivity and, in some cases, revision ideas.

AGNI Online: "Secret Shoes" Originally titled "From a Childhood"
Cimarron Review: "If Every Man Were a Robert DeNiro", "The Catch", & "Hidden Costs"
The Georgia Review: "The New World Deli"
Green Mountains Review: "Exact Life-Time", "Domestic Surrealism II", "Epilogue:" & "Obsolete Organs"
Harvard Review: "Impending Hurricane"
Hotel Amerika: "Voyeur Voyager"
Indiana Review: "Little Bennie Against The World" & "The Missing Thirteen"
Iodine Poetry Journal: "Cherries Out of Season"
MARGIE: The American Journal of Poetry: "Dressing in the Dark"
Mid-American Review: "Pranks & College Literature", "Pockets" & "God in Pasta"
The Ohio Review: "Point A", "The Salvador Dali Exhibit: Rome, 1999", "Cocktail Tree" & "Domestic Surrealism"
Painted Hills Review: "Spring Baseball"
Passages North: "Home Town Chemistry"
Ploughshares: "Escaping God" & "The Whispering Campaign"
Poetry: "Domestic Surrealism: The Late Guests"
Prairie Schooner: "The Ghosts of Luxury" & "Clean"
Quarterly West: "Sober Trees"
Slipstream: "Law & Order" & "Crybaby Blues" Originally titled "Untitled Blues"
Sundog: The Southeast Review: "Math"
TriQuarterly: "Hitting a Skunk at 60 Miles per Hour"
Witness: "Neighborly Love"

"The Ghosts of Luxury" also appeared in *Visiting Frost: Poems Inspired by the Life & Work of Robert Frost.*
"Sober Trees" also appeared in *Poetry Daily.*

Thanks to The Connecticut Commission on Culture & Tourism for a grant which was a great help with completing this book.

Special thanks to Leslie Johnson, Terese Karmel, Wally Lamb, Pam Lewis & Ellen Zahl for their inspiration, encouragement, feedback and good ideas about the poems. Also, without Steve Orlen, not one word of one of these poems would have ever been written.

(photo by Cassandra Kerns)

About the Author

Bruce Cohen's poems and essays have appeared in a wide range of literary publications including *The Georgia Review, The Harvard Review, The Indiana Review, Ploughshares, Poetry, Prairie Schooner, and TriQuarterly*. *Disloyal Yo-Yo* is his first collection of poems; another book of poetry, *Swerve*, is forthcoming from Black Lawrence Press. He is a recipient of an individual artist grant from the Connecticut Commission on Culture & Tourism. Born in the Bronx, New York, educated at the University of Arizona, he now lives with his wife and three sons in Connecticut, where he directs The Counseling Program for Intercollegiate Athletes at the University of Connecticut in Storrs.

LaVergne, TN USA
17 January 2010
170248LV00001B/54/P